ONE NATION UNDER GOD:

# AMERICA'S

# LOST
# DREAM

written by Tom Dooley    illustrated by Bill Looney

First Printing: August 2005

Copyright © 2005 by Tom Dooley. All rights reserved. No part of this book may be reproduced in any manner whatsoever without written permission of the publisher, except in the case of brief quotations in articles and reviews. For information write: Master Books, Inc., P.O. Box 726, Green Forest, AR 72638.

Illustrations by Bill Looney
ISBN: 0-89221-620-4
Library of Congress Catalog Card Number: 2005925561

**Printed in the United States of America**

Master Books

# Acknowledgements

Confession time. Before I became an author I never read acknowledgements. I wanted to get right into the "meat" of the book. Let's face it – all that's going to happen is that a bunch of people whom I will never meet, much less talk to, are going to get praised and thanked by the author. All that back-patting seemed a little too "personal" for me, so I usually just skipped over it to get to the good stuff. I'll do it later.

Things have changed. Now, I'm an author with a lot of people to thank and who deserve the credit. So this is sort of a public apology, an "acknowledgement" if you will, to all the writers whose acknowledgements I never read. Sorry – I repent. A book does not happen by itself. Oh yeah, there's this name on the front, but, the fact is, this book (any book) would not, could not happen without a lot of people involved. Writing a book gives new meaning to the old phrase, "no man is an island." If you ever write a book I pray that you get to work with a publisher like the New Leaf Publishing Group. Their unrelenting love for creating great books keeps the "bar of excellence" at the highest level. Besides, God knew I would need lots of grace.

There's an old saying (by whom I don't know) that a good marriage is the closest we come to Heaven on Earth. Melanie, you are the "wind beneath my wings." I love you with an undivided heart. Thank you for giving me the space to dream and write. Without your patient, loving encouragement there would be no book. I'm beginning to understand what the Bible means when it says, "the two shall become one flesh." I really don't know anymore where I end and you begin.

If you are old enough to have figured out that life is all about relationships then you have learned something about true wisdom. This book exists because of old friends like Steve Farrar and the late Dick Halverson, former U.S. Senate Chaplain, both of whom imparted to me a fervent love of God and country. Many years ago Billy Graham appointed me to be the narrator/announcer for his books and television ministry (you can imagine how that changed my life). Dr. Graham's integrity and his unwavering, single-minded devotion to Christ has been like a compass always pointing to true North (he always insisted that I call him "Billy" but I never could). I also wish to thank David Barton and Peter Marshall for awakening me and my entire generation to the importance of knowing more about America's true history and Godly heritage. My hope is that this book will serve to instill in you a deeper love for this great land and for the God whose unseen but obvious hand has been and continues to be behind it all. Finally, thank you for reading my acknowledgements. Now you won't have to apologize to me when we meet.

Abraham Lincoln

Thomas Jefferson

John Quincy Adams

James Madison

Christopher Columbus

Andrew Jackson

John Adams

# Freedom!

Long ago and far away deep in the misty and forgotten memory of our nation there was born a dream of a sovereign state where people would be free and only God would be their king. This dream of "One Nation Under God" meant freedom from the rule of human monarchs and tyrants. Across the ocean the mightiest empire in the world scoffed at the dream and sought to crush the dreamers, and so, a great Revolutionary War ensued. Like David facing Goliath the dreamers stood before the giant foe. After a long and bloody war, to the amazement of the watching world, the ragtag defenders of the dream prevailed and the new nation came to be. The United States grew . . . guided, protected, and strengthened by God's benevolent hand. Over time there came other threats that sought to crush the dream. There was a terrible Civil War, two world wars, and several smaller ones, but the dream lived on."

Slowly, inexorably, a long season of spiritual apathy crept over the land like a fog. The fire of the dream was extinguished and the nation forgot. Where would we be today if not for the courage and convictions of the dreamers of yesteryear whose words and deeds inspire us now to reawaken the dream? Throughout our history many of our greatest leaders believed that America's future was inextricably linked to America's faith. George Washington stated, "It is the duty of all nations to acknowledge the providence of Almighty God." Abraham Lincoln declared, "All the good from the Savior of the world is communicated through this book. But for the Bible we could not know right from wrong." John Quincy Adams wrote, "The highest glory of the American Revolution was this: it connected in one indissoluble bond, the principles of civil government with the principles of Christianity." John Adams stated, "Our Constitution was made only for a moral and religious people. It is wholly inadequate for the government of any other." James Madison said, "We have staked the future of all of our political institutions upon the capacity of mankind for self-government according to The Ten Commandments of God." Thomas Jefferson asked, "Can the liberties of a nation be secure when we have removed the conviction that these liberties are the gift of God?" Andrew Jackson urged, "Go to the Scriptures! The joyful promises it contains will be a balm to all your troubles." Christopher Columbus admitted "For the execution of the journey to The Indies I did not make use of intelligence, mathematics or maps. It was The Lord who put it into my mind." With these inspiring words let us now begin our journey in search of *One Nation Under God: America's Lost Dream.*

# New Horizons

$\mathcal{L}$et us return to a former time in a far away land when people did not enjoy such freedoms as are found in this great nation today, and let us learn of the first dreamers. In the early 1600's, almost two centuries before the United States adopted its constitution, two main factors existed that fostered the birth of the dream. The first was the state of the Church that existed in England at that time. As a result of the Protestant Reformation of the previous century, the Church of England, also known

Sailing to a new world

as the Anglican Church, had come to be the dominant religion in England. A group known as the Puritans within the Church complained that the Church was not completely reformed and sought to "purify" it.

A smaller group within the Puritan movement was even more critical of the religion and felt that conditions within the Church were irreparable, choosing to leave and worship God in the way they believed was right. The members of this smaller group were called Separatists.

To worship outside the Anglican Church within England was illegal. Many Separatists were arrested and imprisoned. Some had their homes seized; some were branded on the face to show them as heretics; a few were even hanged. They began to dream of sailing to the New World across the ocean where they would be free to worship God according to their interpretation of Scripture, but emigration to America was very expensive and the dangers of the wilderness and its inhabitants made others stay behind.

Of the hundreds of Separatists who shared the dream only 37 would actually sail. There were 65 others on board the Mayflower including Puritans, ship's crew, and hired help. A second ship, the Speedwell, had to turn back to England after about 300 miles because of leaks. No matter what their identity may have been upon departure all who made this epic voyage would come to be identified as "The Pilgrims."

$\mathfrak{H}$alfway across the Atlantic severe storms with lightning, hard rain, and high winds threatened to sink the small ship, causing at least one main beam to crack. Jacks were used to insert support beams to hold it. One passenger was almost swept overboard during a fierce storm. By the time of arrival in America, two souls had perished on the crossing, but two had been born on the way, so the total of 102 Pilgrims made it across the ocean. However, the storms had blown the ship off course far to the north of its intended landing site. The Mayflower came in near the mouth of the Hudson River to the peaceful waters of Cape Cod, in present-day Massachusetts.

$\mathfrak{S}$ixty-five days out from Plymouth, England they spotted land. The Lookout shouted "Land Ho! Land Ho!" It was 7 o'clock in the morning on November 9th as shouts of joy and tears of relief mixed together in a great wave of emotion. The Pilgrims had made it to the New World and were now far out of reach of the Church of England and the king. Here they could build homes, raise children, and begin to form "One Nation Under God." What was once only a dream . . . was now real.

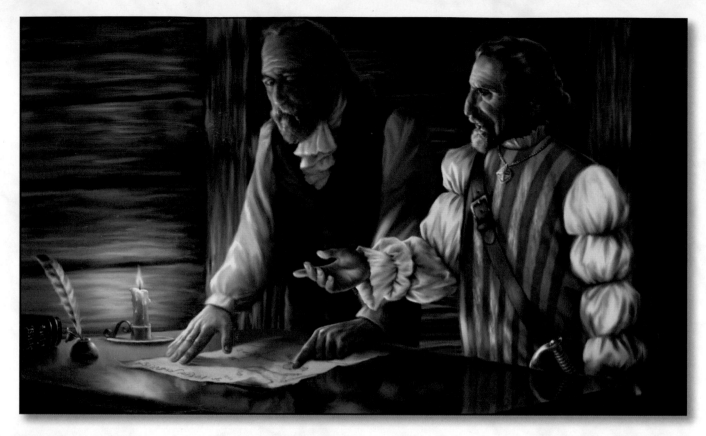

William Brewster, the elder of this tiny band of Pilgrims, sought out the Captain of the Mayflower, Christopher Jones, and asked him what part of North America they were approaching. Jones told him the long, low shore was known to English sailors as Cape Cod because of the great fishing in its nearby waters. However, this was not welcome news for Brewster. The winter season was just beginning which meant they had to make landfall soon.

The agreement negotiated with the king and his ministers in England directed them to settle below latitude 41, roughly the northern border of present day New York. After much debate, and an encounter with shoal water that almost sank the ship, they decided to ignore this legal technicality and proceed with the landing.

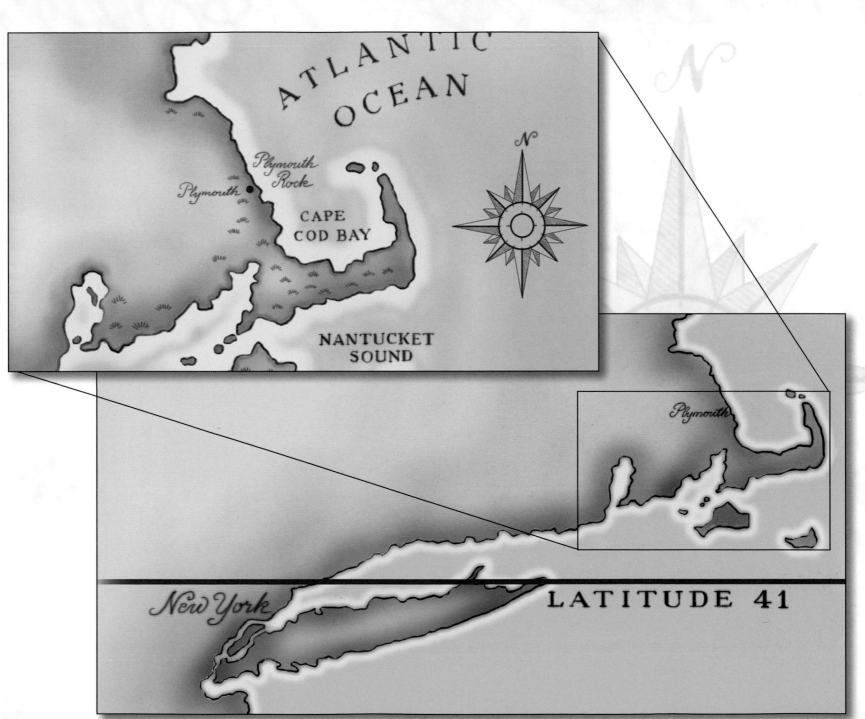

ATLANTIC
OCEAN

*Plymouth Rock*

*Plymouth*

CAPE
COD BAY

*N*

NANTUCKET
SOUND

*Plymouth*

*New York*

LATITUDE 41

Right away there was an uprising among several of the hired hands who did not share the Pilgrim's religious convictions. They had simply signed on in exchange for passage to the New World where they would pursue their own dreams. They banded together and told the leaders that because they were landing in the wrong place they were "freed from the government of any man." They made it clear that they would take no orders from anyone and planned to go off on their own.

They did not hesitate to suggest that if anyone tried to stop them there could be bloodshed, but even if they avoided violence, a split in the group would be disastrous. Every able-bodied man was needed to get shelter up before the snow began to fall. The leaders debated on how to deal with this crisis.

Among them was an ex-soldier, Captain Miles Standish. He and several other men were the only ones who had weapons and were preparing to use force against the malcontents.

William Brewster, chose a different course. He began to draw up an agreement that would establish equality for every man aboard. Brewster's document came to be known as the Mayflower Compact and was the forerunner of our Declaration of Independence and Constitution. It contained such powerful historical phrases as "all men are created equal" and "government by the consent of the governed."

The Mayflower Compact said, in part,

We, whose names are underwritten . . . by the grace of God, . . . having undertaken for the glory of God, and advancement of the Christian faith, and the honor of our king and country, a voyage to plant the first colony in the northern parts of Virginia, do by these presents, solemnly and mutually, in the presence of God and one another, covenant and combine ourselves together into a civil body politic, for our better ordering and preservation, and furtherance of the ends aforesaid: and by virtue hereof do enact, constitute, and frame, such

just and equal laws, ordinances, acts, constitutions, and officers, from time to time, as shall be thought most meet and convenient for the general good of the colony; unto which we promise all due submission and obedience.

The Mayflower Compact was so well crafted and clear that there was not one dissenter when the document was adopted by the group.

The Mayflower dropped anchor and they came ashore at Plymouth Rock. Greeted by the local natives, they were welcomed to this new land as friends. Many national historians look upon the Pilgrim's landing as the beginning point of our nation.

$\mathfrak{A}$ close bond developed between the Europeans and the Native Americans. The locals helped the newcomers prepare for the coming winter. Even so, the next few months proved tragic; of the 102 Mayflower passengers who made it to America, only 51 survived that first, extremely harsh, New England winter . . . but the dream lived on.

# New Challenges in the New World

On July 4, 1776, perhaps the greatest document in the history of the United States was signed in Philadelphia, the Declaration of Independence. With this single page a new nation was born under God. Our forefather's trust in Almighty God was the only guarantee for the price of freedom outlined in the Declaration's final line which states the following; " . . . with a firm reliance on the protection of Divine Providence we mutually pledge to each other our lives, our fortunes, and our sacred honor."

On that fateful day at the Pennsylvania State House, what is now called Independence Hall in Philadelphia, the best men from each of the colonies sat down together to tell our British fatherland "No more rule by Redcoats!" This was a fortunate hour in our nation's history, one of those rare occasions in the lives of men when we had greatness to spare. These were men of means, most of whom enjoyed much ease and luxury in their personal living, but they considered liberty so much more important than security that they were willing to risk everything for the dream.

$\mathcal{I}$n the 150 years that had passed since the founding of that first colony at Plymouth, the growing population, mostly from England, had begun to think differently than their cousins back home. The class distinctions that prevailed in Europe (lords, dukes, earls, etc.) were not a part of life in the colonies. England began to pass laws and impose taxes in order to regulate the flourishing business in America, and by the 1760's, the colonists felt that the British Parliament was treating them unfairly. Resentment began to grow.

In 1774, the First Continental Congress convened in an effort to unite the 13 colonies as one body in addressing England's injustices toward them. For more than a year, representatives from the colonies sent letters and emissaries to England trying to reconcile their differences with the mother country, but to no avail. Tension continued to mount until April of 1775, when the "shot heard 'round the world" started the American Revolution. Ironically, at the start of the conflict, very few colonists wanted to go to war with England.

$\mathfrak{H}$owever, the bullying, uncompromising attitude of Britain helped rally more and more colonists to the cause of independence, even though very few believed that the 13 colonies could ever withstand the might of the superpower. British troops targeted those they considered leaders of the rebellion. Of the 56 men who signed the Declaration of Independence, few were long to survive.

Five were captured by the British and tortured before they died. Twelve had their homes from Rhode Island to Charleston sacked, looted, occupied by the enemy, or burned. Two lost their sons in the Army, one had two sons captured. Nine of the 56 died in the war from its hardships or more merciful bullets . . . but the dream lived on.

Reed

$\mathcal{B}$y 1776, already warring with Britain, the colonies had never officially declared the reasons for going to war, their purpose of separating from England, and their independence. In June of 1776, a resolution was drawn up which stated flatly that these united colonies are, and of right ought to be, free and independent states, that they are absolved from all allegiance to the British Crown, and that all political connection between them and the State of Great Britain is, and ought to be, totally dissolved.

The Continental Congress appointed a committee to draft a declaration of independence in line with this resolution. The original document was mainly written by Thomas Jefferson, and went through many amendments by the committee until it was read in Congress on June 28. The reading was not unanimously well received. Debate was tabled until July 1.

It must be remembered that declaring independence from Britain was not the desire of every colonist. It was not a time of rejoicing and celebration — to break away from the mother country was a very serious and long-considered matter — and so every word and every expression of the declaration was scrutinized and questioned.

Rodney

McKean

No part was accepted lightly, but with all gravity, as these who would be signing their names to the guarantees of "life, liberty, and the pursuit of happiness" for every man were laying their own lives and liberties on the line. The committee's declaration was hotly debated by representatives who were for independence, and those who wanted to stay with England. Even those who wanted independence did not agree with certain sections of the document.

One thing upon which they all seemed to agree was that in order for the declaration to have any power to bolster the unity of the colonies, the vote by the Congress would have to be unanimous. Everyone knew that a declaration of independence would mean a certain and bloody war with England. So, if any one of the 13 colonies was unwilling to assist in the battle, that one colony had the power to stop America's bid for freedom.

Jefferson

On that July 1 in 1776, Congress took a preliminary vote on the resolution for independence. When the votes were tabulated, all 13 colonies had either abstained (the New York delegation was not qualified to vote until a later date) or voted for independence. All, that is, except Delaware. The Delaware vote was split between the two gentlemen present. The third delegate from Delaware was not there.

Caesar Rodney had a malignant, cancerous growth on his face and was so sick with a high fever that he was home in bed unable to attend. The two other delegates from Delaware cast opposing votes. Thomas McKean, who shared Rodney's zeal for freedom, voted for independence while George Reed voted against. Rodney's vote was needed to break the tie or the new nation's dream of independence would be lost.

Thomas McKean sent a messenger on horseback to inform Rodney of the dire circumstances. The messenger arrived at Rodney's house in Dover, Delaware late that night. Upon hearing the news, Rodney rose from his bed, demanded a horse, and began the long night's ride 80 miles to Philadelphia in a blinding thunder and lightning storm. The storm was so severe that most of the roads were washed out or completely blocked by mudslides and downed trees, but Caesar Rodney rode on through the dark night and into the morning, changing horses several times.

He finally arrived at the Pennsylvania State House (Independence Hall) in the early afternoon just as a second vote was being taken. Soaking wet and covered with mud, Rodney clung to his horse, unable to even dismount because of the sheer exhaustion and the fever that continued to rage in his body. He was taken down from his mount and brought inside on a stretcher. Upon entering the Hall of Congress and being asked his vote, Rodney, with all the strength he could muster, replied,

"Sir, as I believe the voice of my constituents and of all sensible
and honest men is in favor of independence and my own judgment
concurs with theirs, I vote for independence."

Caesar Rodney, who had ridden 80 miles from Dover all through the stormy night and into the morning with a festering cancer on his face and sick almost to the point of death, barely survived the ordeal. But in gaining freedom for his countrymen he had selflessly relinquished any chance left to him of going to England for the medical treatment of the cancer that did eventually cause his death. One vote – by one person – had kept the dream alive.

The document was formally passed on July 4, 1776 and on the 8th, the Declaration of Independence was read aloud from the steps of the Pennsylvania State House, after which the Liberty Bell was rung. Years before, the Liberty Bell had been appropriately inscribed with Leviticus 25:10:

*"Proclaim liberty throughout the land and to all the inhabitants thereof."*

The American Revolution had ended in 1783 at the signing of the Treaty of Paris with Great Britain, but the quarrels with Britain would continue over the next 30 years. The iron fist of the British Empire was not about to allow these traitors to the king to live in peace for long. America was too great a prize to lose and England would do whatever it took to regain control over her, but the Americans were determined to protect the dream.

The superpower invaded the United States in two places: from the north out of Canada and on the Atlantic seaboard. Her ships sailed into Chesapeake Bay, and on August 24, 1814, the British attacked Washington. During the intense battle, the White House and Capitol were destroyed. President Madison and his cabinet had to flee the city. Hope dwindled as the English forces advanced. America was once again coming under the power of the British Crown.

$\mathcal{T}$he last remaining American gunship valiantly charged the invaders, sinking at least two of its prized warships. Being smaller and faster than any in the British armada, the gunship managed to evade enemy fire for most of the engagement. However, late that afternoon, with her ammunition gone, the lone ship was attacked by two of the larger enemy vessels and sunk. The entire crew was lost.

The British fleet then moved up the Chesapeake Bay toward Baltimore, Maryland, the third largest city in America at that time. On September 12 they arrived and found a thousand men at Fort McHenry whose guns controlled the harbor. If the British wished to take Baltimore they would have to first get past that fort.

It was just another beautiful September day in the sleepy harbor town when the first British warship unexpectedly appeared out on the horizon. England had successfully attacked Washington just a few weeks earlier and won. Now, the War of 1812 was on Baltimore's doorstep threatening to plummet the tiny country back under the rule of tyranny. The sight of a heavily armed English Naval vessel quickly caused widespread alarm. Soon the entire harbor was filled with them. However, this fight would be different than the one fought in the Capital. The Americans had been preparing for this encounter. They were much better organized and fought more efficiently.

However, five miles outside Baltimore, during their first engagement with the enemy of their freedom, the American forces were soundly defeated. It was a devastating blow. Morale was low and hope began to wane as victory now seemed beyond reach. America was too great a prize for England and they were determined to put these upstart Colonists back in their proper place. The Brits advanced into the city ready to bring the war to a rapid conclusion. But the Americans were dug in and could not be coaxed from their defensive positions. Attacking their fortifications head-on would result in heavy casualties. The British came up with an alternative plan. They would retreat and begin a naval bombardment on Fort McHenry.

On one of the British ships was an aged physician, Dr. William Beanes. A kind and compassionate healer, he had been treating any wounded soldier brought to him – British or American. While dressing the wound of an American in Maryland he was arrested by Redcoats for aiding the enemy and was brought on board England's flagship as a prisoner.

When he heard of the arrest, Francis Scott Key, a lawyer and friend of Dr. Beanes, in an act of incredible bravery and loyalty, borrowed a small boat and rowed three miles out to the flagship to try and negotiate the good doctor's release.

The British Captain was willing, but Dr. Beanes and Mr. Key would have to wait. It was the night of September 13 and the bombardment of Fort McHenry had already begun. From the flagship anchored eight miles away, Key and Beanes could see the American flag flying over Fort McHenry, and as twilight deepened, the night engulfed the flag. They knew the soldiers of the fort would resist – down to the last man – but the old and dilapidated fort was certainly no match for the formidable firepower of the British fleet. But as long as the flag flew, there was hope.

Cannon Ball

Rocket

The British possessed two new types of technology for warfare. The first were fire rockets that were designed to explode into huge fireballs and burn down the wooden structures surrounding the fort. The second was a new kind of cannonball that contained a bomb inside the iron ball. The cannonball had a wick that would be lit and the shooting of it would be timed so that the bomb would explode as it landed. These two new weapons were ferocious and deadly.

   As the British began to unleash them, however, a storm materialized seemingly out of nowhere and a hard rain began to fall. The rain was dousing the fire rockets, putting them out before they landed. The wicks on the cannonballs contained too much gunpowder (a mistake at the factory) causing them to burn much more quickly. As a result, the bombs exploded prematurely – in air – before landing on the fort. With each explosion above the fort, Key and Beanes could see the flag still waving. The British ships attempted to move in closer, but the artillery from within the fort did them too much damage, so they quickly retreated to a safer distance.

The night, the rain, and the thick smoke soon blocked out any view of the flag, and Key and Beanes anxiously waited for the first light of dawn, hoping to see the flag. They must have asked each other many times, "Can you see the flag?" When daylight began to displace the darkness, Francis Scott Key used a telescope to search the sky just above the fort. Suddenly it appeared! Though tattered and torn the flag still flew in defiance of the grueling bombardment. The British fleet began retreating back up the Chesapeake. They had unleashed all their firepower throughout the night and were now completely out of ammunition.

Excited about the news, Key used the only paper he had, a letter he was carrying, and began to compose a poem on the back of it about the "rockets' red glare" and "bombs bursting in air." Think about it. What good are bombs that explode in the air before reaching their target? God had provided a storm with heavy rain that crippled the enemy's war machine and so turned the tide of the battle and the war. Key's four stanza poem was originally titled "The Defense of Fort McHenry." It became popular by its nickname, "The Star Spangled Banner," and in 1931 Congress adopted it as our national anthem. Again, the dream had survived.

# A Nation Torn Asunder

The dream of "One Nation Under God" faced its most formidable challenge not from an outside enemy, but from one that grew within our own borders. We were well on our way to becoming a land of opportunity where the spirit of freedom would grow and expand along with the American frontier, but there was a great unresolved conflict standing in the way of our progress.

The agricultural economy and grand lifestyle enjoyed by those who owned the huge Southern plantations was built and maintained on the backs of slaves. The very idea that a man could own another man or woman like he owned a horse or a steer became a great stumbling block of contradiction in this land of the free.

$\mathfrak{M}$en and women were bought and sold like cattle on the open slave market and often subjected to cruel treatment at the hands of their masters.

Attempts were made to put away slavery peacefully, but in the end the conflict would not be averted by words, by deeds, by compromise, or by laws, although many good men and women attempted to settle it in those ways.

Among them was a humble, plainspoken citizen from Illinois, a self-taught lawyer running for the Senate named Abraham Lincoln. He asserted that the United States could not remain "half-free and half-slave." Lincoln lost that election in 1858, but, in losing, he won. The people could not forget this eloquent man who was the embodiment of the American dream. Two years later they elected him President, but, by then, the time for reasonable words had passed. He wrote, "I know there is a God and that He hates slavery. I see the storm coming. I know His Hand is in it."

And so there came a great Civil War, a war not prompted by an uprising amongst the slaves. They were virtually powerless to do anything to help their own situation, but the conscience of the country could not allow this terrible wrong to endure. We caused it, we allowed it, we had to make it right. And so we did. The Civil War was fought by one race of people to set another race free. It was the deadliest war in our history claiming the lives of more than 500,000 Americans. When it was over the nation had been preserved and the institution of slavery was gone forever.

𝔑ear the end of his life President Lincoln, who had often invoked the name of God publicly, was asked by a newspaper reporter if he was a Christian. Lincoln replied by saying, "Sir when I came to The Senate from the State of Illinois I was not a Christian. And when I became President, still, I was not a Christian. But when I walked the battlefields at Gettysburg it was then that I cried out to the Savior for mercy and forgiveness and he heard my cry and I became a Christian."

Though the war was now officially over, deep hatred and division still walked among us. Retaliation for the Union's victory over the South found its highest revenge when John Wilkes Booth assassinated President Lincoln at the Ford Theatre on the evening of April 14, 1865 while the President's wife looked on in horror.

Though deeply wounded . . . the dream was still alive.

# New Challenges In The Modern World

As we have seen, the dream of being "One Nation Under God" has faced great obstacles along the way, many of which seemed insurmountable at the time, but God intervened to save us and restore the dream. Our history is replete with heroes, like our founding fathers and others, who have been willing to lay down their lives for the dream. Today we face even greater obstacles that seem even more insurmountable. The enemies of the dream still seek to destroy it, but they will never succeed. God is still intervening on our behalf because He still has a divine destiny for America. We don't have to search our past to find heroes, for they are among us today. Jesus said, "Greater love hath no man that he lay down his life for his friends." When those New York City firemen began running up the stairs of the World Trade Center buildings, they didn't know they were responding to a terrorist attack. All they knew was that the building was on fire after being hit by a plane and people on the upper floors desperately needed their help. They went charging up those stairs with no thought for their own safety. Their unflinching bravery, noble loyalty, and unhesitating sacrifice were in keeping with the highest ideals of the American spirit, and we must never forget.

*T*he price of freedom is always paid for with the currency of blood by those willing to lay down their lives for others. If our freedom is to be preserved now, it will require the greatest courage and moral fiber we have ever known. There are enemies both inside and outside our country who are actively seeking to destroy the dream. America needs a new spiritual awakening. We need to wake up and remember the dream. We need to recall who we are as a people . . . what we believe, what we stand for. We have a glorious history and a rich spiritual heritage. It's in our national DNA. Our purpose, our calling, our destiny is to be "One Nation Under God". No, we don't need to go back in time, but we do need to reconnect with the timeless principles of faith in God and love of country and our fellow man. People with strong faith make good citizens. Instead of self-seeking and self-interest groups, we need to return to the time honored maxim of Jesus' Golden Rule, "Do Unto Others As You Would Have Others Do Unto You." We need national leaders who will call us back to the dream. From where will we receive the wisdom, courage, and enlightenment we need to secure our future? Perhaps from one final visit to our past . . . .

# The Voices of Our Founding Fathers

We have often heard it said that America was founded as a "Christian nation." Is that true? If you mean that a person had to be a Christian to be a citizen of this country, the answer, of course, is no. If you mean that the new government exhibited Christian principles in all of its dealings with its citizens, the answer again would have to be no. Slavery would put to rest any argument that the country was following Christ's command to "love one another." It is simply incorrect to say that America was, in her early years, a "Christian nation." However, the influence of Christ and His Word upon the minds and hearts of the vast majority of our founding fathers is undeniable, except by those who purposely distort the truth.

Because of those who have attempted to rewrite our actual history to match their own godless outlook, most Americans today have no idea how vital Scripture was to those who laid the foundation of the United States. The evidence is all over Washington. Visit our Capital and you will see Scripture chiseled in marble on public buildings and monuments everywhere, and thank God it was "chiseled!" If it hadn't been it would certainly be gone by now. In spite of all the clear evidence to the contrary, we're told by the revisionists that our founding fathers were deists, men who simply believed in a "higher power." How 'bout it? All this talk about the "faith" of our founding fathers, is it just hype? A lot of fundamentalist, right-wing, religious propaganda? Let's set the

record straight. Let's allow our founding fathers to speak for themselves. Their words shine like beacon lights into our present day, pointing us in the right direction.

Let's begin at the beginning with our first President – On June 8, 1773 George Washington wrote the following:

"Almighty God, we make our earnest prayer that thou wilt keep the United States in Thy Holy protection and thou wilt incline the hearts of the citizens to cultivate a spirit of subordination and obedience to government and entertain a brotherly affection and love for one another and for their fellow citizens of the United States at large. And finally that thou wilt most graciously be pleased to dispose us all to do justice, to love mercy, and to demean ourselves with that charity, humility and pacific temper of mind which were the characteristics of the Divine Author of our blessed religion. And without a humble imitation of whose example in these things, we can never hope to be a happy nation. Grant our supplication we beseech thee through Jesus Christ our Lord, Amen." Here is the man we call "the father of our country" praying to God in the name of Jesus. So much for "deism."

hat children learn in school today about Washington is mostly myth, like the story about him chopping down the cherry tree. It never happened, but this story did: When Washington was a 23-year old Lieutenant Colonel in the French and Indian War his life literally hung in the balance for two hours. His job was delivering orders from the General to the other officers in the field. He had to be out in the open on horseback during the entire battle. The Indian sharpshooters had been given specific instructions to shoot the officers. The plan worked. Sixty-three of the 86 officers were casualties.

After the battle Washington wrote a letter to his brother describing his acknowledgement of the hand of God that secured his safety. He wrote the following:

"By the all powerful dispensations of providence I have been protected beyond all human probability or expectation. For I had four bullets through my coat and two horses shot from under me. Yet I escaped unhurt. Although death was leveling my companions on every side of me."

Fifteen years later, the Indian chief who was in charge during that battle met Washington and related to him the following account. He said:

"I called to my young men and said, 'Mark yon, tall and daring warrior, himself alone is exposed. Quick, let your aim be certain that he dies'. Our rifles were leveled, rifles which but for you knew not how to miss. Twas all in vain. A power mightier far than we shielded you. Seeing you were under the special guardianship of the Great Spirit. we immediately ceased fire at you. I come to pay homage to the man who is the particular favorite of heaven and who can never die in battle."

God protected the young Washington because He had a plan for his life that included the leadership of this new nation. Throughout our history many of our national leaders have publicly acknowledged our dependence on God's provision, protection, and blessing.

# Notable Quotes from our Past Leaders

### President Coolidge wrote:

"The foundations of our society and our government rests so much on the teachings of the Bible that it would be difficult to support them if faith in these teachings would cease to be practically universal in our country."

### Andrew Jackson said:

"Go to the Scriptures. The joyful promises it contains will be a balm to all your troubles."

Woodrow Wilson said "The Bible is the one supreme source of revelation of the meaning of life, the nature of God, and spiritual nature and need of men. It is the only guide of life that really leads the spirit in the way of peace and salvation."

## On April 30, 1863 President Lincoln wrote:

"We have been the recipients of the choicest bounties of heaven. We've been preserved these many years in peace and prosperity. We have grown in numbers, wealth and power as no other nation has ever grown. But we have forgotten God. We have forgotten the gracious hand, which preserved us in peace and multiplied and enriched and strengthened us. And we have vainly imagined in the deceitfulness of our hearts that all these blessings were produced by some superior wisdom and virtue of our own. Intoxicated with unbroken success, we have become too self-sufficient to feel the necessity of redeeming and preserving grace, too proud to pray to the God who made us. It behooves us then, to humble ourselves before the offended power, to confess our national sins and to pray for clemency and forgiveness."

## Patrick Henry stated:

"It cannot be emphasized too strongly or too often that this great nation was founded not by religionists but by Christians. Not on religion but on the gospel of Jesus Christ."

The two greatest threats America faces today are secular humanism and the theory of evolution. These two belief systems have done more damage to the soul of our nation than any outside enemy. Secular humanism denies any responsibility to the personal God of the Bible. Evolution, which is not science but merely a man-made belief system, has further devalued us as less than God's creatures made in His image. The unfortunate result is through "moral relativism", we have become our own gods . . . and we are paying a terrible price for our error. Without reconnecting to our roots, spiritually and nationally, we will continue to cheat ourselves of our destiny, personally and corporately. We are God's stewards of America as surely as the Jews were the stewards of the Promised Land.

Former Senate Chaplain Dick Halverson wrote, "America's future depends on the people of God being the people of God. Christians have got to be Christians! Our failure to heed and obey God portends destruction, which is why 'judgment begins in the house of God' (1 Peter 4:17; KJV). As representatives of God's kingdom in the world, our failure, our sin deprives the world of the purifying, healing, redeeming influence of righteousness. 'In God We Trust' and 'God Bless America' are phrases that have meaning only to the extent that they have meaning in our hearts, the citizenry. We need the life-giving nutrients of our roots. It is time to begin the pursuit of becoming 'One Nation Under God, America's Lost Dream.' "

# AUTHOR

Tom Dooley is unquestionably one of the nation's top music-radio personalities. His stellar career spans more than 25 years with an impressive résumé of ratings successes at major market stations. Gifted with a voice made in heaven and a remarkable narrative ability, Tom Dooley is a top national "voice-over" talent. Tom began his career in Christian radio while at WFIL-Philadelphia in 1978 with a weekly Sunday morning show called "Alpha Omega." That program evolved over the years into what is now "The Journey," which Tom hosts six days a week from KVTT in Dallas, Texas. Along the way, he has been at some of the biggest stations in the country including WCBS-FM-New York, KHJ-Los Angeles, WFIL-Philadelphia, and KVIL-Dallas, where he still holds the record for midday ratings.

As national program director of CBN in Virginia Beach, he pioneered the nation's very first Christian music satellite radio network, Continental Radio. He has narrated countless documentaries, and his lists of commercials include clients like Radio Shack, Zales Jewelers, GE, and many more. Tom also served as the official "voice" of the Billy Graham Evangelistic Association, narrating many of Dr. Graham's national TV specials and several of his books on tape. Tom and his wife, Melanie, became born-again believers in Christ in 1977, and Tom became an ordained minister in 1996. They have been married 30 years and have three grown children. They live in Colleyville, Texas, with their boxers, Bugsy and Abby.

# ILLUSTRATOR

Dallas–area illustrator Bill Looney is, to use the common vernacular, a "natural." He has painted commissioned portraits and artwork for scores of clients over the past three decades. He is a master of all art–related media including airbrush, oils, acrylics, computer illustration, and watercolor. Bill attended the University of Texas at Arlington and the Dallas Art Institute.

Bill honed his craft for many years in the demanding commercial world of graphic art design and illustration. A Christian since 1974, his desire to use his talents for the Lord led to his close friendship with Christian radio personality Tom Dooley. Having worked on several projects together, *The True Story of Noah's Ark* has been the most demanding and rewarding project so far. He is now employed full–time at MasterMedia working on future biblical productions.

$\mathcal{A}$merica's Lost Dream has been produced into an incredible, 90-minute stage production that features a giant 3-screen multi-image show presented "live" by the author, Tom Dooley. This is a breathtaking spectacle of sight and sound across three giant screens. The huge, animated, panoramic images tell the story of America's Lost Dream in a way that makes an indelible impression on all who experience this dynamic presentation. It is an unforgettable event! If your church or civic organization would like to sponsor America's Lost Dream in your community, call MasterMedia for more information: 1-800-343-7378. See the video demo on our website: www.mastermedia.org

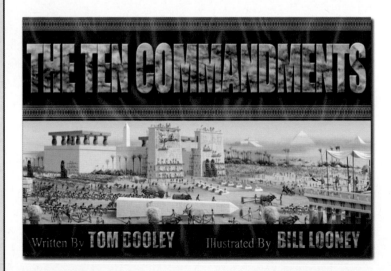

$\mathcal{G}$et ready...here they come...again! The creative team of Tom Dooley and Bill Looney have done it again! Their upcoming book, *The Ten Commandments*, tells the ancient story from a new and fresh perspective. The original storyline follows the biblical narrative but with insights that give new depth and dimension to this epic tale that has become a modern day controversy. As one would expect, Bill Looney's intricately detailed illustrations are superb.